THE NEW IS NOW!

THE NEW IS NOW!

ROSEMARIE SHELLSHEAR

ISBN: 978-1-9650500-5-7
Published by Purelilly Press Publishing
Huntsville, Texas

First Printing, 2025

THE NEW IS NOW!

Living Life Today and Beyond

21 Daily Devotionals

Contents

This book is dedicated to:

Dorothy Ruth Campbell,

my mother

and

Thomas Marcus Shellshear, Jr.,

my husband of 38 years

Forward

Seasons come and seasons go, but one thing I have found about the Lord is that every day with Jesus can be a Bright New Day! No matter what you went through yesterday, today can be the start of a Brand-New Beginning! Each day is a chance to start over!

And though some seasons seem hard and linger on for a long time (and you think it will never end), God has a plan, and as you take His hand, He will guide you into the next place of your destiny.

This is my reality after experiencing a season of caregiving for both my mom and my husband, my two favorite people in the world, and then seeing them graduate to heaven. In the painful transition of "letting go of what was," I began to venture out and try new things (attend schools, seminars) and a restart to speak, teach, and sing once more. Then suddenly I knew it was time to "Dream Again" and start another New Chapter in my life!

And thus, you have this book, "*The New is Now!*" Please join me as we journey together in these devotionals to step into the amazing plan God has for us and have some fun along the way! Let's get started.....

Are you ready?

THE NEW IS NOW!

Rosemarie Shellshear

Behold, I will do a NEW thing.

Now it shall spring FORTH;

Shall you not know it?

I will even make a ROAD

In the wilderness and RIVERS

In the DESERT.

Isaiah 43:19

1

Dream Again

> *"For I know the plans I have for you, says the Lord. They are plans for good and not for evil, to give you a future and a hope."*
>
> *Jeremiah 29:11 (TLB)*

I believe God is saying to His people, *"It's time to dream again!"* God has fresh, new marching orders coming to His believers. New assignments are on the way! Our God is a God of new beginnings!

As we listen to the voice of the Holy Spirit, He will plant new ideas and thoughts into our hearts. Our responsibility is to just stay alert and be ready to walk through the doors that He opens. The best part is that your age is not a factor – nor your weight – nor how you look – nor your income – nor your education. You can be a blessing just like you are!

Did you know God's dream is always tied to helping people? Maybe you had visions of grandeur in the past of being famous or doing something great and making a difference in this life. You still can! But this time, God wants you to shift your thinking and concentrate on making HIS NAME famous. Our prayer should be, *"Lord, who can I bless today? How can you use me to be a blessing to help others and to further your Kingdom?"*

I am so glad the Lord gave us the scripture found in Romans 8:28, *"And we know that all things work together for good to them that love God, to them who are the called according to His purpose."* (KJV)

Perhaps you had a vision of getting married and having children, but your childbearing years are now over. Can you trust that God can use your pain to help someone else who may have experienced the same heartache? And that He can turn your sorrow to joy and give you meaning and purpose in the midst of your circumstances?

Maybe you have lived your dream, but that season is over. Or you may feel that all you have is an elusive dream that always seems just beyond the bend. Don't give up hope. Stay in faith and expect great things from a wonderful Heavenly Father who loves you so much. I love the fact that God can bless us in each season of our journey and helps us to see that our total fulfillment really only comes from knowing Him, not in what we do.

The Lord says in Psalms 37:4 that as we delight ourselves in Him, He will give us the desires of our hearts. We must come to the place where we say, *"Lord, I delight in YOU! What are YOUR desires for my life? Let YOUR desires be MY desires. Let YOUR plans be MY plans."* I have discovered that when God plants His desires in us and we cooperate with Him, His plans always succeed, and we experience great joy!

So, my question for you today is, *"What is GOD'S DREAM FOR YOU? Are you DREAMING WITH GOD?"* Today is the day to open your heart to a new beginning – IT'S TIME FOR YOU TO DREAM AGAIN!

Prayer for Today:

"Lord, let me live the dream you have for me, knowing that when one dream ends, You will always have another. Help me enjoy each season of my life and savor the beauty of today. Encourage me along the way so I can encourage and bless others. In Jesus' Name, Amen."

For the LORD GOD

Is a SUN and SHIELD;

The Lord will give

GRACE and GLORY;

No GOOD thing will He withhold

from THOSE

Who walk UPRIGHTLY.

Psalm 84:11

2

Arise and Shine

> *"Arise, shine; for thy light is come, and the glory of the Lord is risen upon thee. For, behold, the darkness shall cover the earth, and gross darkness the people: but the Lord shall arise upon thee, and his glory shall be seen upon thee."*
>
> *Isaiah 60:1-2 (KJV)*

The time has come for us, as believers, to take our position in the body of Christ and be the mighty warriors God has called us to be. I believe God is positioning His body and launching us out for Kingdom purposes. It is no longer business as usual. Our Heavenly Father sees where we are and knows what He wants us to do.

How do we tap into the purposes of God? By listening to His still small voice and being ready at a moment's notice to step into new ventures as He directs. Get ready to be a first responder to the Spirit's call. We are going to experience the God who does *"exceedingly abundantly above all we ask or think, according to the power that works in us!"* (Ephesians 3:20, emphasis added)

We must remember that it is "His" power and not ours. So we don't need to be afraid to step out when we know He has already commissioned us as believers to *"Go ye therefore, and teach all nations..."* (Matthew 28:19 KJV). And Jesus said, *"I am with you always..."* (Matthew 28:20). It is important to listen for new marching orders in the days ahead.

No matter what you have been going through in the past season (the joys as well as the sorrows), God has been training you in His boot camp to make you *"strong in the Lord, and in the power of His might."* (Ephesians 6:10) And He wants to move us forward as His ambassadors here on the earth.

Know this – that Jesus is coming back for a glorious church, a church without *"spot or wrinkle"* (Ephesians 5:27), a victorious church! We must be willing to step out of the boat and walk on the water as Jesus directs. Yes, the winds and the waves were all around, but Jesus was right there with Peter. And so, He will always be with us.

As one minister said, "Get ready, get ready, get ready!" It's time for the Body of Christ to get up, stand up, and speak up. When we are called upon, all we need to say is, *"Yes, Lord, I'll do it! For your honor and your glory! I'll go to the ends of the earth or to my next-door neighbor. Wherever you lead me, I will follow."*

My brothers and sisters, it's time for us to

ARISE AND SHINE!!!

Prayer for Today:

"Lord, I want Your light to shine through me everywhere I go today. Please help me make a difference in the lives of everyone I meet. Fill me with Your boldness and courage and use me to touch my world for You. In Jesus' Name, Amen."

Your ears shall hear a WORD

Behind you, SAYING,

"This is the WAY,

WALK in it,"

Whenever you TURN to the

RIGHT HAND or whenever

You TURN to the LEFT.

Isaiah 30:21

3

Entering the New Season

> *"Behold, I am doing a new thing; now it springs forth, do you not perceive it? I will make a way in the wilderness and rivers in the desert."*
>
> *Isaiah 43:19 (ESV)*

Stepping into a new season can be both exciting and difficult, all at the same time. You're not where you used to be (the familiar, the old), and yet you're not where you're going to be (your next assignment, the new). You know God has something more for you than what you are experiencing now, but how do you get through the wilderness to your Promised Land?

In the book of Exodus, the children of Israel were on their way to Canaan (their land of milk and honey), but there were giants who had to be conquered before they entered. What are your giants today -- fear, insufficient funds, lack of direction?

Do you know that you do not have to conquer these giants alone? As a Christian and follower of Jesus, you have a big GIANT

KILLER living on the inside of you, the HOLY SPIRIT. He will speak to you, help you conquer each giant, and also make some valuable discoveries along the way. So, what are those discoveries? I'm so glad you asked. Here are a few to consider:

Discovery No. 1 –Totally depend on God.

Friends, if we haven't realized it by now, we're not going anywhere worthwhile without God's leadership, guidance, help, and strength. We simply cannot make it through life without Him. Jesus said, *"I am the way, the truth, and the life."* (John 14:6) Our God is a God who makes a way where there seems to be no way. He *"opens doors that no man can shut and shuts doors that no man can open."* (Revelation 3:7-8, paraphrased)

Discovery No. 2 – Enjoy the journey.

We must learn to be content during the transition period, knowing that God won't leave us there forever. Complaining like the children of Israel will assuredly slow down the process. Also, something wonderful happens when our eyes see new sights we were too busy to see in the past season.

Discovery No. 3 – Let go of the past (victories and defeats).

We simply cannot move into the new season if we're hanging onto the old.

Discovery No. 4 – Be open to new adventures!

This is a new day! God has great plans for His children! He might be preparing you to do something you've never done before. He might be shifting your paradigms. Our God is so creative and innovative. He loves to help us move from "out of the box" thinking, where life used to be, to a fresh new mindset and an entirely different season.

So, when does our adventure begin? It begins today! As we leave the wilderness to enter our Promised Land, we can rest assured that God is with us through our journey to new avenues and new mountain heights. He will remind us to smell the roses along the way and leave the past behind.

Get ready, my friend!

Your new season is just around the corner!

Prayer for Today:

"Lord, keep my hope alive and my expectations high for the next adventure you have for me. Give me ears to hear and eyes to see which direction the Holy Spirit is leading me. Help me move in sync with Your timing and give me markers along the way to show me I am moving in the right direction. In Jesus' Name, Amen."

And WHATEVER you do,

Do it HEARTILY,

As to the LORD

And NOT to MEN,

Knowing that from the LORD

You will receive the REWARD

Of the INHERITANCE;

For you SERVE the Lord Christ.

Colossians 3:23-24

4

What's In Your Hand?

> *"Whatever your hand finds to do, do it with your might..."*
>
> *Ecclesiastes 9:10*

Step up to the plate and get ready to bat! God has something fresh and new for you to do that will astound even YOU! I believe He is saying now is the time to come out of your comfort zone and enter the new season – a season just yearning to tap into your potential and use those gifts and talents that have been waiting to be released for this day and hour.

God wants to use YOU to display His glory (His manifested presence) in the earth realm in a greater measure than ever before. He has definitely saved the best until last! Signs, wonders, and miracles are going to flow through YOU, His people! The key is to be available in every gifting and calling.

You might say, *"I'm not so sure I have that many gifts, talents, abilities, and most definitely, I don't have a lot of resources to draw from."* So His question to each one of us is, *"What's In Your Hand? What do you have that I can use? Are you willing to offer it up to be used for My glory?"*

Moses had a shepherd's rod that God used to part the Red Sea. David owned a slingshot and five smooth stones that brought down Goliath. A little boy gave Jesus his lunch, consisting of five loaves of bread and two fish, and saw Jesus multiply that lunch to feed thousands.

From time immemorial, God has been the mastermind at taking what the world calls ordinary to do the extraordinary. And His supply never runs out. The enemy always tries to get us to focus on what we don't have, how bad the economy is, how bad everything is on the world scene, and he wants us to lose sight of the fact that our God is still in control (and always will be). He will never leave us or forsake us. Jesus said over and over, *"do not worry... my peace I give to you...let not your heart be troubled."* (Matthew 6:25, John 14:26-27, John 14:1)

Meanwhile, as we continue to cast our cares on the Lord, He says I have something for you to do. Will you take what you have and use it to touch a lost and dying world? How about sending a text message on your cell phone with a word of encouragement to one of your friends? Or maybe you like to bake? Most people like cookies, and that could be the very thing to let someone know that Jesus cares for them.

My next-door neighbors are from India, and I picked up the cutest little (stuffed animal) bear to give to their young daughter just to let them know that I was thinking about them. It didn't cost much, but it was my way of expressing love to their family.

Now is the greatest time that we can reach out to touch those around us! People are listening. They are hungry for the Lord! They are hurting. They see what is happening on the world scene.

WHAT'S IN YOUR HAND? Give it to the Lord and watch Him use it for HIS GLORY!

Prayer for Today:

"Lord, I am available for You to use my gifts and talents. I will be alert and listening to You, Holy Spirit, for creative ways and ideas of how to bless others with what You have given me. Let me put smiles on people's faces and lift the hearts of those around me. In Jesus' Name, Amen."

And He SAID to THEM,

"Go into ALL the WORLD

And PREACH the GOSPEL

To every CREATURE."

Mark 16:15

5

What's Love Got to Do with It?

> *"Beloved, let us love one another: for love is of God; and every one that loveth is born of God, and knoweth God. He that loveth not knoweth not God; for God is love."*
>
> *I John 4:7-8 (KJV)*

Have you ever thought, *"Gee, I really would like for God to use me, but I'm not a pastor, nor do I have a lot of training."* And sometimes we can make it so hard. But do you know one thing we all have deposited in us if we have accepted Jesus as our Savior? It's the love of God, and we simply need to share His love with others, and He can use us in powerful ways!

Did you know that God can use you to change someone's life forever? Yes, that's right! YOU! There's someone out there that needs you – your touch, your smile, your love. You can be God's hand extended to a world out there that's hurting – a world that needs to know that someone, somewhere cares. And we know someone who does care.

JESUS CARES. And He works through wonderful people like you and me – people who want to see other people filled with hope and smiling again. Well, you might say, *"I'm hurting myself. I need someone to minister to me."* But did you know that if we get our eyes off ourselves by helping someone else, God will make sure that the seed we sow comes back to us.

I heard a pastor say his mother told him, *"Son, be nice to everybody, because everybody is going through something."* It's true. There's probably not one person in this world who has it all together. People need encouragement. They need the love of God. And that's where we come in.

The Bible says, *"...the love of God is shed abroad in our hearts by the Holy Ghost..."* (Romans 5:5 KJV). As a believer in Jesus Christ, love is not something we have to muster up in our own human efforts. God puts His love in us, and He will activate us to show that love as we go through our daily routine. I've found a good way it can begin is simply by noticing people. Did you know people love to be noticed, acknowledged, and validated?

Sometimes, if you're like me, you get so busy in your day that you forget to notice people. A personal example is when I'm in a hurry during checkout at the grocery store line, and I fail to notice the checker because I have my head down the entire time putting my groceries on the conveyor belt. The Holy Spirit told me one day that I needed to do better and at least "look up!" And then acknowledge them by saying something like, *"How is your day going?"* or even *"Thank you for helping me. I hope you have a good day!"*

People love to be noticed! And complimented! One checker told me she had a headache, and I said a "very quick" prayer for her! (Remember, at the grocery store line, you have to be "quick" so you don't get them in trouble for stopping what they're doing.) She was so touched and moved that I cared. And there are many more ways to show God's love everywhere you go.

Another way to show God's love is by SMILING! When you see someone, give them a GREAT BIG SMILE! It doesn't cost anything, and you will find something remarkable. THEY SMILE BACK! So go ahead. Here's your assignment for today. Give a smile to as many people as you can and see how your spirit is lifted as well.

So...

"What's Love Got to Do with It?"...

Everything! ... Everything.

Prayer for Today:

"Lord, let Your love flow through me by the power of Your Holy Spirit to encourage someone today. As I interact with the people I see, let them know You care about them, have not forgotten them, and want to help them with every one of their needs. In Jesus' Name, Amen."

And the KING will ANSWER

And say to THEM,

'Assuredly, I SAY to YOU,

Inasmuch as you DID it

To one of the LEAST of THESE

My BRETHREN,

You did it to ME.'

Matthew 25:40

6

It's Time to Release Your Story

> "Go home to your friends, and tell them what great things the Lord has done for you, and how He has had compassion on you."
>
> Mark 5:19

Everyone has one... a story, that is... except your story is different from anyone else's, and there is someone out there who needs to hear it.

Now the adversary, that old devil, will tell you that no one wants to listen to your 'lil' old story. *"Who are you anyway? Save your breath. Look at you. You're still in process."* But don't you dare believe him! He's lying to you. You, as a born-again believer, have some testimonies inside of you that God wants to release in this hour.

Has someone ever told you about a particular situation he (or she) was facing, and you thought, *'Wow! I remember going through a* similar experience myself. At that time, I could not even imagine how I would make it through. But then God did a miracle for me, and I not only survived, but I can attest to the faithfulness of God!"

You suddenly realize that God wants to use you to be a "Barnabas," an encourager to the person He has sent your way, and maybe even pray for them. The Bible says in 2 Corinthians 1:4 that God "...comforts us in all our troubles, so that we can comfort those in any trouble with the comfort we ourselves receive from God." (NIV)

My friend, my question to you is this. Has God healed your body, saved your soul, seen you through the death of a loved one, or brought you through any kind of difficulty? (I believe we can all say a hearty, "Amen!") Then it's testimony time! Here's the good news! You do not have to be a preacher or get on a platform to share your experience. The world is your platform!

God has called each one of us to minister in our sphere of influence... to give hope to those around us. And He will send someone who is drawn to a person like you (with your intellect, your physical appearance, etc.). They will listen to you, whereas they might not listen to someone else, especially if you have been through a similar experience.

So what are you waiting for? The Bible says to "Always be prepared to give an answer to everyone who asks you to give the reason for the hope that you have." (I Peter 3:15 NIV) A very important key is to listen to what the other person is saying first... to be interested in their needs... and then allow the Holy Spirit to speak through you!

I believe God is going to use you and all of us in so many ways! Get ready to bring God's drink of water to a thirsty soul! And as you refresh others, God will bring someone to refresh you! (Proverbs 11:25 KJV) We serve an awesome God!

Prayer for Today:

"Lord, as I listen for your promptings to share my story of how you saved me, helped me, or blessed me in any way, give me Your "Holy Spirit boldness and anointing" to encourage others as I speak. Let them know how much you love them and will be there to help them, too, as they call out to You. In Jesus' Name, Amen."

Let brotherly LOVE

CONTINUE.

Hebrews 13:1

7

What I Like About You

"By this all will know that you are My disciples, if you have love for one another."

John 13:35

S everal days ago, I was thinking about the people in my life and how they have blessed me – family, friends, clergy, neighbors, doctors, etc. And I believe the Holy Spirit gave me the idea, *"Why don't you tell them. Everyone needs encouragement, and they may not even know how I am using them."* In the past, I have never been one to "brownnose," and I actually find it very distasteful and phony. But I do believe in honoring people by giving genuine compliments and praise.

Let me share a few examples of how the Holy Spirit launched me into action. One friend, Debby, experienced the death of her husband of many years, the love of her life, while they both fought the good fight of faith to keep him alive. I watched this precious woman, whose heart was aching, continue to come to church, tears and all, and pray for others as she walked through the grieving process. What an inspiration it was to me to see that she did not allow any bitterness or resentment to creep in and kept on loving God and loving people, even though things didn't go her way. Then the Holy Spirit said to me, *"Why don't you tell her?"* And so I did, and she was remarkably surprised. [On a side note, sometimes we think no one is watching us, but that simply is not true. Our life is a constant testimony to those around us.]

Then there is the story about my friend Keith. On one occasion, when he saw my mom, Keith waved and smiled and called her by name and made Mom feel so special. She could not believe he remembered her, and his friendliness made her feel about 10 feet tall! Keith has a ministry of hospitality, and as he greets others, he is a blessing. I was delighted to tell him to keep passing out those smiles and friendly "hellos!"

These are just a couple of examples, and I could name so many more. It is always nice to pass out kudos to your spouse for the wonderful ways he or she helps you, as well as give our thanks to waiters, grocery store clerks, and just about anyone who has blessed us or helped us in any way. We find in scripture that Jesus went around doing good, healing those who were oppressed, and just making people feel special. He is our role model, and He says, *"As the Father has sent Me, I also send you."* (John 20:21)

So, who in your life has blessed you? What, in particular, do you like about them? Go tell them now. Give them their flowers while they are living. I believe this will not only bless them, but it will bless you as well, and you will see God use you in a special way.

Prayer for Today:

"Lord, help me verbally express my appreciation and thanks to people who bless me in my life's journey. May the words I speak let them know what a difference they have made in my life. May I also be a blessing and show Your lovingkindness to those around me. In Jesus' Name, Amen."

Blessed be the GOD and FATHER

Of our Lord JESUS CHRIST,

The Father of MERCIES

And God of all COMFORT,

Who comforts US in all our

TRIBULATION, that WE may

Be ABLE to comfort THOSE

Who are in any TROUBLE...

II Corinthians 1:3-4a

8

We Need Each Other

> "... pray for one another..."
> James 5:16
>
> "Bear one another's burdens, and so fulfill the law of Christ."
> Galatians 6:2

Several years ago, I was praying on my church's Prayer Team, and a beautiful single businesswoman approached me to pray for her. She had moved to the city I was living in at the time and stated she had been attending my church for one year. In her words, *"I love the preaching and the worship, but I am dying of loneliness. I come in and go out every Sunday, but I have no fellowship – no other Christians to talk to, and there just has to be more for me."* I had to agree.

Could it be the answer is found in small groups where everyone can participate and maybe even give "a psalm, a hymn, or a spiritual song?" (Colossians 3:16) – a place of belonging where people pray for one another and truly care for each other, and they know each other's name!

I don't know about you, but I love going to church – to hear the preaching, worship the Lord by singing praise songs, and rub shoulders with other believers. However, I do believe there is also a need to connect with one another on a smaller scale.

My "late husband" Tom and I were privileged to serve in a large church for many years. I remember when I first walked in the door, I thought to myself, *"How will I ever fit in here? No one knows me. I'll just be one of the masses."* But God has a wonderful way to connect us. We found several small groups, and God began to weave us into His tapestry for ministry. For me, it was the choir, the worship team, and teaching Bible classes. For Tom, it was leading the Host Ministries and eventually becoming the Director of Church Development. But the best place we connected with other believers was in our "Home Group," which met in the home of a church member.

What is a Home Group? For us, it was a smaller group out of the larger body of believers who fellowshipped together once a month – potluck meals, prayers, a small devotional, and lots of love. This group made our "very large" church seem small. Every time we attended church, we would somehow bump into these people, and they would brighten up our day because we actually felt like we knew somebody – somebody who cared! We laughed together, and we cried together.

During one heart-wrenching event, these people were the hands and feet of Jesus to us. This happened when our 30-year-old daughter-in-law suddenly passed away, leaving 2 children (a one-month-old baby boy and a 4-year-old toddler). The Holy Spirit used our Home Group to minister to us and comfort us in a way that we cannot even describe. Just knowing they were there for us helped us to bear the load.

Founding Pastor John Hagee of Cornerstone Church in San Antonio, Texas, said the secret to the success of his church is found in the hundreds of small groups that meet each week throughout the city of San Antonio. These are not just "bless me" clubs (or cliques) but places where ministry can actually happen to Christians as well as to non-Christians on an individual basis.

This year, I am praying the Lord will cause us to draw close to one another, and everyone will find their place of fellowship and ministry in the body of Christ, and not just be spectators who attend church every Sunday, but truly find their place of belonging.

Prayer for Today:

"Lord, I ask you to connect me to the people in a small group where we can love and pray for each other, share our burdens, and fellowship on a regular basis. Put me in the place You have designed for me, where I will not only be a blessing but receive a blessing as well. In Jesus' Name, Amen."

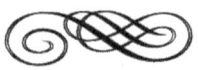

To EVERYTHING

There is a SEASON,

A time for every PURPOSE

Under HEAVEN.

Ecclesiastes 3:1

9

Focus

WHY ARE WE HERE?

WHY ARE WE DOING WHAT WE ARE DOING?

> *"So teach us to number our days, that we may apply our hearts unto wisdom... that we may rejoice and be glad all our days."*
>
> *Psalms 90:12-14 (KJV)*

Several years ago, I had the privilege of mentoring a young Christian woman. On a somewhat regular basis, we would meet for lunch, and I would pour into her what the Holy Spirit gave me for that day. Since I knew this would only last for a season, I asked the Lord, "What is the most important principle you want me to leave as a deposit in her life?

And here's what the Lord said. Tell her, "On a periodic basis, no matter what task we're performing, all of us need to assess our journey and ask ourselves these questions: '*Why am I here? Why am I doing what I am doing?*'

In life, it is so easy to lose our focus. So let's delve into this a little deeper. Today, can we be honest with ourselves and ask these questions?

1. Why am I here?
2. Why am I doing what I am doing?
3. Am I on the right track?
4. Do I feel energized by the Holy Spirit, or am I just going through the motions?
5. Is what I'm doing producing fruitfulness or just busyness?
6. Am I being blessed? Is it blessing anyone else?
7. Is this season over, or just a difficult place where I'm being trained and stretched and using my spiritual muscles?
8. Does God have something new for me?
9. What's really important here? Am I so caught up in the "nitty gritty" details or off on some "bunny trail" that I've lost sight of the big picture?

My friend, God loves you! He wants all of us to live a fulfilled, abundant life... a joy-filled life with meaning and purpose. We can sing all year long, "JOY TO THE WORLD! THE LORD IS COME!"

He came to save the world, to show us His love, and for us to become a conduit of His love to a world that desperately needs Him. In order to do that, all of us need to live a life of enthusiasm and walk with exuberance and vitality!... living by faith, knowing we're in His perfect will and doing what He has called us to do.

So today, in the hustle and bustle and busyness of life, will you take a brief moment to say to your Heavenly Father, "May Your

Kingdom come. May Your will be done on earth as it is in heaven. May Your focus be my focus, and Your plans my plans."

Prayer for Today:

"Lord, let me live each day focused on Your meaning and purpose for this season of my life. And when I feel a shift coming to move into another season, I ask you, Holy Spirit, to help me "let go of the past" and to guide me in the transition to the new plan that You have for me. In Jesus' Name, Amen"

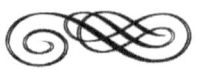

Casting ALL your CARE

Upon HIM,

For He CARES

For YOU.

I Peter 5:7

10

Overload, Unload, Reload

> *"For My yoke is easy and My burden is light."*
>
> *Matthew 11:30*

I n today's society, the pressures of life can seem overwhelming. People are suffering from real issues and real problems. Some might even ask the question, *"Where is God in all of this? I thought His yoke was easy and His burden was light. I cry out to Him, but the answers seem delayed in coming."*

Believe me, I can identify. Several years ago, I was under extreme pressure – smiling on the outside and pretending everything was fine. But it wasn't fine. I was stuffing my feelings and trying to act like "Miss Super Christian." Because, after all, I thought if a person was actually an on-fire, dedicated follower of Jesus, they could just soar through life on wings as eagles.

After developing stomach problems, I sought the Lord for His pathway for my healing. This seemed to be a slow process and took several months. But, praise God, I am doing well and want to share my process for healing.

One evening, while in much pain, a friend invited me to attend a small "home" gathering of believers where we just worshipped the Lord and sang praise songs. While singing, the Lord spoke three words to me: "OVERLOAD, UNLOAD, RELOAD." I knew exactly what He meant.

1) OVERLOAD – "You're too overloaded – too many cares, concerns, your schedule is too full."

2) UNLOAD – "I want you to learn how to cast those cares (on Me, your Lord). Also, you need to unload some things from your schedule. You're too busy."

3) RELOAD – "by using the Word of God and prayer. Find scriptures on healing and quote them every day." There is tremendous power in speaking God's Word. God said He would also help me "reload" my scheduling.

So, I began to get up earlier every morning. Before I left for work, I took time to quote healing scriptures, pray, cast my cares on the Lord, and then take a few minutes to listen for His daily marching orders. What a marvelous, miraculous thing the Lord did for me. Little by little, I could see a breakthrough until I was healed from those severe stomach issues.

Maybe you, too, are struggling and burdened down. God never intended for you to carry such a heavy load. As you seek Him, He will show you His pathway for your healing. And it may be different from someone else with the same issue. Listen for His specific plan to fit you. He designed you, knows how to fix you, and His desire is to meet your needs and shower you with every blessing! He truly is an amazing God! My prayer is that you will always experience the abundant life He promised to give you, and your yoke will be easy and your burden light.

Prayer for Today:

"Lord, I know it is not Your will for me to carry such heavy burdens. When I feel "overloaded," help me "unload" by streamlining my schedule and casting my cares on You. Help me "reload" by reading Your Word, praying, and listening to Your still small voice. Today I want to experience Your presence, power, and peace in my life. In Jesus' Name, Amen."

WAIT on the LORD;

Be of good COURAGE,

And He shall STRENGTHEN

Your HEART;

WAIT, I say,

On the LORD!

Psalm 27:14

11

Be Still and Know

> *"Be still, and know that I am God..."*
>
> *Psalm 46:10*

Has the Lord ever asked you to do something that absolutely made no sense to your natural mind? And you knew that to get to your Promised Land, you would have to obey Him? He might say, *"Lay down that position, task, or job because I have something else for you to do."* And you say, *"Okay, God. What is it? I'll do it."* And then all you hear is silence.

"What kind of game is this, God? You can go ahead and tell me. Just let me know where we're going and what you want me to do. I can take it from here." Still nothing. No word. Nothing.

In Genesis 12:1, the Lord spoke to Abraham to leave where he was and go to a land *"I will show you."* If you're like me, you want 55 confirmations, an angel to speak from heaven, and the entire plan from start to finish. And I'm not saying it's not good to take a "pause" before you "jump ship" too fast, so you don't make some gross mistake. But when those confirmations do come that say leave the old and you're sure, you think, *"What next? What is my next? Now that I've left my old place and everyone thinks I'm crazy, what's next?"*

When the Lord asked me to leave a particular place, the only Word He gave me was *"Be still and know."* I didn't want that. I wanted, *"Be still and GO..."* to wherever we are going! But everywhere I went for the next year, I kept hearing and seeing the words *"Be still and know."*

I admit, sometimes I must get comfortable not knowing and just following the Lord. And if you're like me, it's hard to be still... and wait... I hate waiting. Because, absolutely, I am a "take action" person. It makes me feel "stupid" to not know where I am going. *"How will I prepare? How will I know when I get there?"*

This is where my faith must kick in... and yours, our faith in the Lord and His promises. If God brought us this far in our lives, and we know He did, He promised to take us to the finish line. So, every day we get up and listen and get excited because we know our "next" will be better than our "last." Why? Because the Bible says He takes us from "glory to glory," and from "faith to faith!" And faith pleases God!

And waiting doesn't mean doing nothing. It means trying new things, reading new books, meeting new people, and believing that as we move in our daily routine, God, through His Holy Spirit, moves too. He will get us to our place called "There," and we can know that our "stillness" before Him will lead us to our next place of amazing fulfillment.

Prayer for Today:

"Lord, this season of waiting is not easy for me. Help me to be still and know that you are God, and remember you have everything under control. In this pause from "here to there," keep my faith alive in Your Word, knowing that You began a good work in me and promised You will finish it. In Jesus' Name, Amen."

I will INSTRUCT you

And TEACH you

In the WAY you should GO;

I will GUIDE you

With My EYE.

Psalm 32:8

12

God's Master Plan

> *"The steps of a good man are ordered by the Lord..."*
>
> *Psalm 37:23*

There are no accidents in the life of a Christian. Our steps are ordered by the Lord, and He has a Master Plan. Sometimes we experience unexpected twists and turns that seem to steer us off course, but in the grand scheme of things, we must believe that the God who calls us will help us to stay on course, give us courage to face the day in which we live, and see us through to the finish line.

In a Master Planned Community, every detail is thought of carefully by a Master Builder... location of the sidewalks, the green belts, the swimming pools, the golf course, tennis courts, and even the mailboxes must be uniform. And let's not forget the color coordination of the landscape and foliage.

God has a Master Plan for each one of His children, and I believe He is painting a picture of our lives. Some of the colors we see on our canvas are bright and vibrant, while others are more subdued, but in order to make a beautiful painting, we find that there must be a blending of both colors.

As a child, do you remember putting together puzzles with those great big pieces? I don't know about you, but those puzzles always seemed easy for me. But then I moved on to the 1,000-piece puzzles, and my love for puzzles soon diminished. It was always hard for me to get just the right fit, and my patience level was definitely not developed in that area.

How about you? Does your life sometimes look like a 1,000-piece puzzle, and you're not sure where the next piece will fit? *"Lord, should I go this way or that way? Am I trying to squeeze a puzzle piece in a place where it really does not belong? What is the next piece in my puzzle?"*

There are many scriptures found in the Bible that talk about God's guidance and fitting together the pieces of our lives, but one of my personal favorites is found in Proverbs 3:5-6 – *"Trust in the Lord with all your heart, and lean not on your own understanding; in all your ways acknowledge Him, and He shall direct your paths."*

Trust is a really big issue with God. If you're like me, sometimes praying and saying words of faith come easily, but believing and waiting for the answer can seem like an eternity. *"Lord, I believe; help my unbelief!"* is a battle we all face from time to time (ref. Mark 9:24).

A great way to keep our faith alive during those times of waiting is to remember how faithful God has been in the past. At just the right time, the Holy Spirit whispered (sometimes thundered) to us the next step in our journey. Our Master Planner seemed to put just the right color on our canvas while at the same time fitting our puzzle piece together. He will come through for you again. He's still the same God. Trust Him today as He paints your Masterpiece, and God's divinely orchestrated plan unfolds for you!

Prayer for Today:

"Lord, let the pieces of my life come together in Your timing and Your way. Help me to trust You along the journey, and when it seems I've lost my way, please steer me back on course. In Jesus' Name, Amen!"

But those who WAIT on the LORD

Shall RENEW their STRENGTH;

They shall MOUNT UP

With WINGS like EAGLES.

They shall RUN

And NOT BE weary

They shall WALK

And NOT FAINT.

Isaiah 40:31

13

Never Give Up

> *"And let us not be weary in well doing: for in due season we shall reap, if we faint not."*
>
> *Galatians 6:9 (KJV)*

Whether you're in a season of transition or just remaining where you are, have you ever been through a battle, whether it was spiritual, physical, or mental, and you said to yourself, *"That's it! I've had it! I quit!"* For those of you who have never been in that place, I commend you. But for us who are willing to pull the mask off and be real, we admit that in extreme pressure, quitting has sounded like a viable option.

Think about it! Just rest and sit back and let someone else take over. You've done enough. No one appreciates you anyway.

Did you know that God appreciates you! He's sitting in the grandstands of heaven and cheering for you; Jesus is interceding for you, and the Holy Spirit living inside you is encouraging you to press on. Don't listen to the lies of the enemy who's trying to "steal, kill, and destroy." It's time to get back up and move into the secret place of the Almighty (also known as your prayer closet) and let the Holy Spirit minister a fresh Word to you.

So how can we get rid of *"Stinkin' Thinkin'"* when our hope, joy, and peace seem to be on a roller coaster ride? Just because we face tough times doesn't mean we're out of the will of God. In fact, it might mean we're right on track... in Texas lingo, we're right "smack dab" in the middle of God's divine purpose. Whoever told you the Christian life would be smooth sailing? I'm sure it wasn't the Apostle Paul or Moses, or Jesus! Yet they saw through the eyes of faith that they were on a mission, commissioned by God Himself. And so are you!

Don't you dare give up! Your greatest days are just around the corner! So, if you're like me, you might be asking the following question: *What did I do to deserve this trial I am facing?* I'm so glad you asked, because you need to realize that God trusts you, and He has been training you up to this point to use your spiritual muscles against the powers of darkness. You are pushing back the kingdom of darkness in certain areas in order to promulgate the Kingdom of God. The great news is that you are not alone.

The Divine Creator of the universe is there to gird you up and strengthen you for the journey! I may not understand how, but that is where faith comes in. He promises over and over in His Word that He will be with us in our times of trouble.

So if I give up now, will my assignment go unfinished? Will someone else come in to do my part? Only God knows. My beloved friend, God is counting on all of us to stay the course. As we do, we will begin to see the victorious hand of God move in powerful ways in our midst.

The Bible says He always causes us to triumph in victory in Christ Jesus! (2 Corinthians 2:14) So now it's time to get back up!

Go look in the mirror and be the mighty conqueror God made you to be!

Prayer for Today:

"Lord, please help me and sustain me when I feel like giving up. When the battle gets too heavy, give me the strength to endure. I know You are in this battle with me, and "I am more than a conqueror" with You on my side. Please send angels to help me and prompt other believers to gird me up and pray for me until I get to the other side of this trial. In Jesus' Name, Amen."

Your WORD is a LAMP

To my FEET

And a LIGHT

To my PATH.

Psalm 119:105

14

⚜

Eye Has Not Seen

"But as it is written:

'Eye has not seen, nor ear heard,
Nor have entered into the heart of man
The things which God has prepared for those who love Him.'

But God has revealed them to us by His Spirit. For the Spirit searches all things, yes, the deep things of God."

I Corinthians 2:9-10

D o you have a personal, lifetime scripture? This would be a passage from the Bible that the Holy Spirit sends your way periodically to encourage you or to prepare you for what lies ahead. I do, and I would like to share it with you.

The text is found in I Corinthians 2:9-10 and states, *"But as it is written: "Eye has not seen, nor ear heard, nor have entered into the heart of man the things which God has prepared for those who love*

Him." But God has revealed them to us by His Spirit. For the Spirit searches all things, yes, the deep things of God."

Over and over in my spiritual journey, the Holy Spirit has given me this passage to encourage me and basically reassure me that I am still on His radar screen. My spiritual antennas now go up because I know this is where His "logos" or "written Word" becomes a "Rhema" or "revealed Word" to me.

The Bible then becomes ALIVE! I can almost see the text jumping off the page and landing straight into my heart! Why did He send me this Word? I believe it was to prepare me for the days ahead. Let me share three examples of when this started.

The first time this amazing scripture dropped in my heart was while I was driving Mom from Houston, Texas, to San Antonio, Texas. The purpose was to get her to the hospital for her sister, Joyce's, upcoming surgery. I should have known something was different when, a week before, while working at my desk, the Holy Spirit told me, "I want you to drive your mom to San Antonio." Being newly saved at the time and not familiar with the voice of the Spirit, I didn't think much about it because my mom had always been afraid to drive long distances. But, on the other hand, this was strange because the surgery was only classified as "minor" surgery.

Well, before the surgery, my mom and her sister, Joyce, reminisced about "old times" and laughed and laughed like teenagers, never knowing that this would be our last visit with "my Aunt Joyce." Three days later, Joyce died, which was a shock to all of us. After that, at Joyce's funeral, my grandfather gave a "spontaneous" Word from the Lord that contained... you guessed it... MY SCRIPTURE... I Corinthians 2:9-10. As he spoke those "specific words," my spiritual antennas went up again! I thought, "Wow! I wonder why I keep hearing these verses?"

The third time this scripture came to me was upon arriving back home from San Antonio, from the funeral. Coming into my house, I heard my phone ringing. A friend on the other end said the Holy Spirit prompted her to get up at 4:00 a.m., write a song, and told her that I was supposed to sing it. What were the words? .... you guessed it! .... I Corinthians 2:9-10. My Scripture! (THE THIRD TIME IN A WEEK! WOW!) I was in awe! Not only did I sing it, but I recorded that song many years later.

So you might ask me, *"What does all of this have to do with me?"* I am so glad you asked because I want to share this scripture with you! Did you know that God has many wonderful things in store for you! Your eyes haven't seen it; your ears haven't heard it, and your mind can't even conceive the wonderful plans God has for you! Listen for His voice. He will reveal those plans to you by His Holy Spirit and His Word... yes, even the deep things of God... His marvelous and wonderful "Revealed Word" to YOU!

Prayer for Today:

"Lord, I love you, and I thank you for this Word and for all the wonderful things you have planned for me. As I walk through this day, help me hear Your voice and reveal to me Your "specific" Words as well as the "deep things" you want me to know. In Jesus' Name, Amen!"

Now to Him who is ABLE

To do EXCEEDINGLY

ABUNDANTLY

Above all that we ASK or THINK,

According to the POWER

that works in US...

Ephesians 3:20

15

Suddenlies and Surprises!

> *"Jesus said to him, 'If you can believe, all things are possible to him who believes.'"*
>
> *Mark 9:23*

Have you ever prayed and believed for something in the past, and the answer came in a way you were not expecting? Suddenly, you discovered God had another idea, and His plan is always better than ours!

In Jeremiah 29:11, we find the Lord saying, *"For I know the plans I have for you, says the Lord. They are plans for good and not for evil, to give you a future and a hope."* (TLB) So be encouraged, my friend! Don't lose heart or lose faith if your current situation does not line up with your expectations. God has a bigger plan, and He is always full of surprises!

Don't you love to see the smile on other people's faces when they receive a "surprise" gift? And then to see the joy that gift brings. What a blessing! Did you know that your Heavenly Father also loves to surprise you?

Many "surprises" and "suddenlies" are found in the Bible! Take Ruth's story, for example. I'm sure it was an emotional upheaval to Ruth when she lost everything... her husband, her income, her home. But then she moved from Moab to Bethlehem, as a support to her Mother-in-Law, Naomi. And what a surprise to Ruth when she started gleaning in the fields of a wealthy Landowner named "Boaz," and suddenly one day, Boaz asked Ruth to marry him! Talk about "rags to riches!" How exciting! Only God can arrange a surprise like that!

And what about David? One "normal" day, he is out in the field tending sheep when his Father called him in, and the Prophet Samuel anointed David as the next King of Israel! Wow! That was both a suddenly and a surprise all in the same day! Hallelujah!

Never forget that God loves to bless His children. He is a good God! In Numbers 6:23-26, God told Moses to say to Aaron, the Priest:

"Speak to Aaron and his sons, saying, 'This is the way you shall bless the children of Israel. Say to them:

The Lord bless you and keep you;

The Lord make His face shine upon you,

And be gracious to you;

The Lord lift up His countenance upon you,

And give you peace.'"

You may have been through some "rough patches" in your life, but believe that good things are on the way!

So, my word to you today is that whatever you are facing, put your hope and faith in God. ONLY BELIEVE! Expect His blessings, and He will meet your every need and give you the desires of your heart. Get ready to open those surprise packages He has for you! What's that? I think I hear your doorbell ringing now!

Prayer for Today:

"Lord, keep my expectations high when I pray, knowing that You will answer me in Your perfect timing and Your way. Encourage me and even send others who will stand in faith with me. Then I know You will help me enjoy my life in the meantime as I continue to trust You for the outcome. In Jesus' Name, Amen."

I DELIGHT to do Your WILL,

O my GOD,

And Your LAW

Is within my HEART.

Psalm 40:8

16

Moving Forward

LESSONS FROM ESTHER

"For if you remain completely silent at this time, relief and deliverance will arise for the Jews from another place, but you and your father's house will perish. Yet who knows whether you have come to the kingdom for such a time as this? Then Esther told them to reply to Mordecai: 'Go, gather all the Jews who are present in Shushan, and fast for me; neither eat nor drink for three days, night or day. My maids and I will fast likewise. And so I will go to the king, which is against the law; and if I perish, I perish!'"

Esther 4:14-16

One morning, I was having my quiet time with the Lord, and I had just finished my Bible reading about Esther. As I was sitting, listening to the Lord about "how to move forward from my last season," I believe the Lord gave me this revelation. But first, let me give you this very brief summary for those of you who don't know about Esther:

The Book of Esther is the story in the Bible of a Jewish woman, a captive and an orphan from Jerusalem, who becomes queen of Persia and saves her people from annihilation.

Without giving you the entire history of the Book of Esther (you can read that for yourself), here are some observations the Lord gave me about Esther's story. Maybe these are good principles we can apply to our own lives:

1. Esther did not come from ideal circumstances, but she took one step at a time. She did not have to have the whole picture.
2. She was willing to go through a "preparation season" before she was selected to be queen.
3. She had beauty, but there were a lot of beautiful women she was competing with. But the Lord chose her because He knew she would be faithful to her God and do what He told her to do. She was obedient to God, even though it could cost her life, but she believed God would protect her.
4. She had influence, but she always used that influence to do what God wanted her to do. She was God's ambassador and did not try to do her own thing.

I believe Esther is a good role model for us to follow as we continue to move forward to live our lives today and beyond. And her life is a wonderful example of how God can raise up even the most "unlikely person" to do great things for Him. The question is, *"Are we willing to be that one?"*

Prayer for Today:

"Lord, help me to remember Esther's example to take one step at a time and go through the necessary preparation to be who You want me to be. May I endeavor to look my best in my appearance, but always knowing that the real, true beauty comes from within. Help me to be faithful and obedient in my daily walk with You and use my influence to do Your will and not my own. In Jesus' Name, Amen."

How God ANOINTED

Jesus of Nazareth

With the HOLY SPIRIT

And with POWER,

Who went about DOING GOOD

And HEALING ALL who were

OPPRESSED by the DEVIL,

For GOD was WITH him.

Acts 10:38

17

Shift the Atmosphere

> *"But you shall receive power when the Holy Spirit has come upon you; and you shall be witnesses to Me in Jerusalem, and in all Judea and Samaria, and to the end of the earth."*
>
> Acts 1:8

Did you know that you have been endued with power! That's right! YOU! After you have prayed and asked Jesus to come into your heart and fill you with His Spirit, the Bible says you have been endued with "power!" The Greek word for "power" is "dunamis" or miracle, mighty working power! Think about it! Dynamite, explosive power is on the inside of you! To do what? To do the works that Jesus did!

Jesus said in John 14:12, *"Most assuredly, I say to you, he who believes in Me, the works that I do he will do also; and greater works than these he will do, because I go to My Father."* What in the world could be greater works than Jesus did? What did He do? He healed the sick, raised the dead, cast out devils, commanded storms to be still, and so much more! What could be greater than that? I believe He was talking about "greater in numbers."

For you see, when Jesus was on this earth, he was only "one" person, and He said in John 16:7, *"Nevertheless I tell you the truth. It is to your advantage that I go away; for if I do not go away, the Helper [Holy Spirit] will not come to you; but if I depart, I will send Him to you."* So this "Helper" is now on the inside of YOU to do the same works that Jesus did! You house the very presence of God on the inside of YOU! But you must plug into that power and release it for that power to do any good!

So, when you go into a place or a room and you see the forces of darkness trying to rule, you have the power of the Holy Spirit on the inside of YOU to shift that atmosphere! For example, if someone does not feel well, you can offer to pray for them and release God's miracle-working power into their body! (Remember, it is His power, and not yours. Always pray "in Jesus' Name" and in His authority, and how do we know we have the right to do that? Because he has delegated to YOU and to ME the right and the authority to use His Name and do the works that He did!)

If a storm is coming and you see dark clouds forming, you can rise up and speak to that storm and say, "Peace Be Still," just like Jesus did! Well, you might say, *"What if it doesn't work?"* Well, I say, *"What if it does!"* If Jesus said it, and He did, what do I have to lose if I go in faith and speak to that storm? Jesus said, *"And these signs will follow those who believe..."* (Mark 16:17 NKJV). But you must believe! And it doesn't cost anything to believe. What do you have to lose?

So every day, go into your "Jerusalem," your sphere of influence, and use your God-given power to shift and change your atmosphere and bring the Kingdom of God from heaven into the earth! You've got the Power! Now use it for His honor and His glory and change your world for Jesus Christ!

Prayer for Today:

"Lord, anoint me with fresh fire and a fresh infilling of Your Holy Spirit today so I can make a difference in my world. I want to shift the atmosphere everywhere I go to bring the rule of Your Kingdom that's in heaven down to this earth! I am excited about how you are going to use me today, and I look forward to being a blessing everywhere I go. In Jesus' Name, Amen!"

But Jesus LOOKED at them

And SAID to them,

"With MEN this is IMPOSSIBLE,

But with GOD

All things are POSSIBLE."

Matthew 19:26

18

Steppin' Into Your Destiny

> *"Blessed is she who believed, for there will be a fulfillment of those things which were told her from the Lord."*
>
> *Luke 1:45*

As we move forward into the "New is Now," we expect God to give us "new vision," and that may require giving birth to something we've never done before. Let's look at four women and their season of giving birth.

1. *Mary, Mother of Jesus – Birth of a Dream – Luke 1:26-38 – Just Say "Yes!"*

When the angel of the Lord came to Mary, he said she was "highly favored," and the Lord had chosen her for a special and specific assignment – to give birth to the Son of God. Wow! That must have been a shock! But what a magnificent privilege! And the Bible says she wondered how that could be since she was a virgin. We know from scripture the Holy Spirit overshadowed her as

He impregnated a seed inside her, and He will do the same with us. *He will plant an idea, a dream, a prophecy, a vision on the inside of us.*

But just as Mary had to *accept that assignment* as she said, *"Be it unto me according to Thy Word,"* we will also need to say *"Yes"* to carry that dream to fruition -- no matter the cost, the stigma, or the responsibility. But just as Mary had Divine help, we can expect Divine help from the Holy Spirit as well.

2. *Hannah, Mother of Prophet Samuel – Delayed But Not Denied – I Samuel 1*

Hannah, who desperately wanted a child, for some reason couldn't conceive, and the devil would torment her through her sister, Penninah. I'm sure that Hannah was disappointed and wondered, *"What about me?"* But even though Hannah's dream was delayed, she wasn't denied. *She had to persevere.*

What did she do? She prayed until she got the victory, and gave birth to Samuel, but also many more children (dreams). (And sometimes the Lord will give us "spiritual children" when we don't birth children in the natural.) But even though our dream may seem delayed, we must *persevere and keep standing in faith until we see that vision or dream come to pass.*

3. *Jochebed, Moses' Mother – Protect Your Dream – Exodus 2:1-10; Numbers 26:59*

Jochebed had to protect her dream (her son, Moses) because Pharaoh was having all the boy babies killed at that time. What did she do? She made Moses an ark of bulrushes and floated him down the river, where he was rescued by Pharaoh's Daughter, who raised Moses as her own son.

We will need to protect our dream, too! _Watch over it, nurture it, and don't be too quick to tell everyone about it._ Remember the old saying, _"Loose lips sink ships!"_ which can be true of our dream too!

Then Moses' Mother was allowed to nurse Moses, but only was with him _"for a season,"_ and eventually had to give her dream (Moses) to Pharaoh's daughter to raise. We need to realize that we may only have our dream _"for a season"_ also.

4. _The Shunammite Woman – Death and Resurrection of a Dream – 2 Kings 4:8-37_

The Shunammite Woman's long-awaited son, _her dream, died,_ but she believed God would _resurrect her dream._ And God did just that! You may have been through the death of your dream, too – a divorce, loss of a loved one, a betrayal, or feeling you're too old, but did you know that _God can resurrect your dream in a "new way!"_ He can bring someone or something else! And we know that _"nothing is impossible with God!"_ Expect God to bring you new hope today and breathe new life into your spirit! He is a great God!

Prayer for Today:

"Lord, when you plant a dream in my heart, let me quickly say "Yes!" Help me to persevere in faith if there is a process, and it seems like my dream has been delayed or denied. Help me to protect my dream, holding it only for a season, knowing that if that dream should die, You will always have another. In Jesus' Name, Amen!"

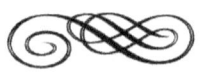

Go therefore and make DISCIPLES

Of all the NATIONS,

BAPTIZING them in the NAME

Of the FATHER

And of the SON

And of the HOLY SPIRIT...

Matthew 28:19

19

Finding Your Team

> "After these things the Lord appointed seventy others also, and sent them two by two before His face into every city and place..."
>
> *Luke 10:1*

Many people feel like they are off on an island by themselves and have no sense of community with others. We know some solitude can be beneficial, especially our quality time of being alone with the Lord each day in prayer, journaling, and Bible reading. But sometimes too much "alone time" can produce extreme loneliness and even despair.

I believe "being in community" is God's idea, and it is important for us to find our tribe, our group, our team, where we can connect with others. And then not only will we receive from them, but we can truly be a blessing to them as well. And I realize that it's not always possible, for various reasons, to be on a team, and sometimes you might be in between your team "season."

But if you don't have a team right now, don't give up. Keep looking! Trust that God will lead you. If you have, you probably figured out by now that it's important, besides having the right Team, to have just the right Team Leader.

Have you ever seen a great Team Leader – a person who has a special knack for taking a group of people and forming them into a cohesive unit? People usually love that person; they love to be on his/her team, and together they accomplish more than they ever would on their own.

Having said all that, have you ever thought about what makes a great team? If you're like me, you don't want to be on any old team. You want to be on a great team! A winning team! A team where everyone pulls together and shares their part of the load – a team that has fun and enjoys the task at hand with common goals.

Some have stated that T-E-A-M means Together, Everyone, Achieves, More, and I like that, but I made up my own list. Here are some attributes I feel constitute a great team:

T-rust   In God first, in your Team Leader, and in each other.

E-nergy   Excitement, and motivation to get the job done.

A-ssist   Where all those on the team have a heart to serve.

M-aster   God's Spirit leads the team.

Did you know that Jesus formed a team of 12 men while He was living here on this earth? Why? He was the Son of God. Did He really need their help? You may have your own opinion on the matter, but I believe the Bible lets us see that Jesus was training them and teaching them so these 12 men could reach out and invite others to be on the same team. The Jesus Team. Jesus said, *"As the Father has sent Me, I also send you."* He also said, *"Go into all the world and preach the gospel..."* (John 20:21, Mark 16:15)

Did you know that those of us who have asked Jesus into our hearts never have to say we don't have a team? We are on a BIG team, the best team there is -- known as the Body of Christ. And Jesus is the BEST TEAM LEADER you could ever find. He has left us the most wonderful MANUAL, called THE BIBLE, to go by.

And so, if you have never accepted Jesus into your heart and been invited to be on our team, I want to ask you.....

"Will you be on our Team? ... the Jesus Team!"

I promise. You will always be glad that you did!

Prayer for Today:

"Lord Jesus, thank you for inviting us to be on Your Team, the Most Wonderful Team in the entire world. Thank you for dying for us on the cross and forgiving us of our sins so we could have eternal life in heaven with you and live our best life right now on this earth. Help us to remember to invite others to be on Your Team. Amen."

If you have not accepted Jesus in your heart, please pray this prayer:

"Dear Heavenly Father,

I know that You have a plan for my life, because You created me and You love me. You created heaven to be my eternal home with You. Forgive me of all my sins, failures, and my past. I believe the blood of Your Son, Jesus, cleanses me from all sin. I repent of my sins and invite You, Jesus, to come into my heart and be my personal Savior. Thank You for saving me, according to what the Bible tells me – whoever calls on the Lord shall be saved. Amen"

Welcome to our Team! The Jesus Team!

If we LIVE in the SPIRIT,

Let us also WALK

In the SPIRIT.

Galatians 5:25

20

Dig A New Well

LESSONS FROM ISAAC

"Then Isaac <u>sowed in that land</u>, and <u>reaped in the same year a hun-</u>
<u>dredfold</u>; and <u>the Lord blessed him.</u> The man <u>began to prosper</u>, and
<u>continued prospering</u> until <u>he became very prosperous</u>; for he had
possessions of flocks and possessions of herds and a great number of
servants. So the Philistines "<u>envied him</u>." Now the Philistines had
"<u>stopped up all the wells</u>" which his father's servants had dug in the
days of Abraham his father, and they had "<u>filled them with earth</u>."
And Abimelech said to Isaac, "<u>Go away from us</u>, for you are much
mightier than we."

Genesis 26:12-16

When God says it's time to "break camp" from your last place, and you say goodbye with a good attitude, looking forward to today, we think it will be "smooth sailing," and in many places it is. But then, in some instances, there can be some "bumps and bruises" along the way as we try to find "Our New Place Called There." Let's see what Isaac did to navigate these hurdles.

During Isaac's life, there was a famine in the land where he lived, and the Lord told him not to relocate to Egypt, but to stay in Gerar. So, Isaac stayed and sowed in Gerar, and as you can see in the scripture, Isaac prospered. But Isaac needed water, so he decided to use the wells Abraham, his father, had dug. The only problem was that the Philistines, because of envy, had stopped up these wells and tried to claim them as their own. The bottom line was that they really didn't want Isaac there in the first place.

As we are moving forward into the new and beyond, not always, but sometimes our well might get stopped up too by circumstances or people. But we don't want what people say or do to drive us from our "destined place" either. So what do we do? Maybe Isaac's situation can give us some insight as to what to do. But first, let me name the wells:

1. "Esek" – Contention or Strife (Genesis 26:19)
2. "Sitnah" – Hatred or Enmity (Genesis 26:21)
3. "Rehoboth" – Spacious (Genesis 26:22)
4. "Shebah" – Good Fortune (Genesis 26:32)

If you read the entire chapter of Genesis 26, you will find that when Isaac's wells were stopped up, rather than staying there and fighting, he just kept on moving to dig another well. Finally, he came to a well called Rehoboth/Spacious that he was able to use (without contention), and then to dig another well called Shebah/Good Fortune.

So, what can we learn from the life of Isaac?

1. Not everyone liked him when they saw him prospering. They threw dirt in his well and rejected him.
2. When his wells were stopped up, he chose to relocate and dig another well. He was a peacemaker.
3. He was also persistent in moving forward despite his opposition and never sought revenge. He realized any rejection was a sign of God's favor on his life, and that God wanted him to carry his belongings to a more "fruitful land."
4. Finally, he found his place of favor, and God blessed him there.

As we move into the NOW, sometimes we might find our well gets stopped up, too. And believe it or not, not everyone is going to like us wherever we go, and that's okay because God will train us along the way to see how we will respond. We always want to be led by His Spirit, choose to stay in peace with a good attitude, and then see if He wants us to stay there (and fight those battles in prayer) or just move on to a more "spacious" place or even to another place of "great blessing." As we face these challenges, may the Lord lead us in our response.

Prayer for Today:

"Lord, as I move forward each day, I am expecting your favor and for my well to stay unstopped. But, if I should find that my well has been stopped up, please give me wisdom as to whether I should stay or move on. Help me stay in peace and exhibit Your love to those around me. Even though at times it might not be easy. I know You will help me respond in a Godly way. In Jesus' Name, Amen."

And lastly,

when all is said and done...

Be anxious for NOTHING,

But in EVERYTHING by PRAYER

And SUPPLICATION,

With THANKSGIVING,

Let your REQUESTS be made

Known to GOD...

Philippians 4:6

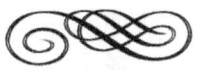

...and the PEACE of God,

which SURPASSES

all understanding,

will GUARD your HEARTS

and MINDS

through Christ Jesus.

Philippians 4:7

21

Remember the Lord

> *"Have not I commanded you? Be strong and of good courage; do not be afraid, nor be dismayed, for the Lord your God is with you wherever you go."*
>
> *Joshua 1:9*

Have you noticed that as we go through life's day-to-day journey, a challenge will come our way that tries to upset our "applecart" – a storm, a crisis, a nuisance – something that tries to steal our peace? We must determine beforehand what our response is going to be.

Will we remember to trust God and experience His power or go into a state of agitation, fear, or panic? When something like this happens, I have found this is the perfect opportunity to be a doer of the Word, exhibit our faith, and see God's glory.

This morning, I experienced a small test – my house air conditioner was not working. Ugh! Texas heat in the middle of summer! And, of all days... on a Sunday. There have been times in the past when I would have "freaked out" and started murmuring and complaining. *"Why does this have to happen to me? Oh, brother! Another expense."* Yada, yada, yada!

But praise God! Even though I am still growing in this area, I have been training in the school of the Holy Spirit, and I want to share with you what I did to walk in victory and maintain my peace. And maybe this will help some of you.

The first thing I did was to inquire of the Lord by praying and asking for His help and wisdom according to Proverbs 3:5-6, which says, *"Trust in the Lord with all your heart, and lean not on your own understanding; in all your ways acknowledge Him, and He shall direct your paths."*

After that, I quoted the Bible, personalizing it, and followed this plan of action:

1. I declared that *"No weapon formed against me shall prosper..."* *(Isaiah 54:17).*
   I also stated, *"This is going to work out for my good because Romans 8:28 states, 'All things work together for our good because we love God and are the called according to His purpose.'"*
2. I remembered the times God had seen me through challenges in the past.
3. I thanked Him that the answer was on the way.
4. I stayed in peace. Jesus said in John 14:27, *"Peace I leave with you; My peace I give to you...[YOU] Do not let your hearts be troubled and [YOU] do not be afraid."* (John 14:27, paraphrased) It's up to each one of us to determine to walk in peace.

Well, I was able to locate an air conditioning technician, which is not easy to do on a Sunday. He showed up in short order, the system was fixed at a reasonable rate, and the best part is that I was able to extend the love of Jesus to the technician by praying God's blessing over him.

So remember, the next time a challenge or crisis comes your way, Jesus is there for YOU! He loves you and will never leave you nor forsake you! Remember to call out for His help and watch Him work on your behalf. His power is always available to those in need.

And so, my friend, I leave you with this word:

Remember, remember, remember...

Prayer for Today:

"Lord, when a challenge comes my way, help me remember to turn to You first for Your help, guidance, and wisdom. Please give me Your peace and direct me to the best plan of action. I also ask You to show me the right people to assist me in solving this problem. In Jesus' Name, Amen!"

CHANGE YOUR LIFE
WITH ONE PRAYER

(YOUR MOST IMPORTANT DECISION)

If you would like to invite Jesus to come into your heart today, pray this prayer! I promise you will never regret it and will be so glad that you did!

Dear Heavenly Father,

I know that You have a plan for my life, because You created me and You love me. You created heaven to be my eternal home with You. Forgive me of all my sins, failures, and my past. I believe the blood of Your Son, Jesus, cleanses me from all sin. I repent of my sins and invite You, Jesus, to come into my heart and be my personal Savior. Thank You for saving me, according to what the Bible tells me – whoever calls on the Lord shall be saved. Amen!

In closing, my prayer for you…

Thank you for joining me on this 21-day journey. I will be praying for you that the rest of your life will be the best of your life, and God will shower you with His richest blessings!

In Jesus' Name!

Love,

Rosemarie

www.ingramcontent.com/pod-product-compliance
Lightning Source LLC
Chambersburg PA
CBHW061704120626
46550CB00003B/1088